Sean Hannity's theocracy;

Plus,

Virgin Mary LIVES!

By Mark David King

Purchase all of my books on Lulu.com—

Here are the titles:

How to practice White Magic

About Britney Spears and male genitalia—an anthropological treatise

Werewolf Slut

The Season of Tara

Dana Dickson battles Lindsay Lohan: Jelly Roll's Poem

www.myspace.com/mark16715

Live free or die!!!

INTRO:

Jelly Roll is a boy barely thirteen;

Still, concerning the Drug War he is keen;

Plus, he's the ultimate human writing machine,

Sharing the philosophy of Tom Paine's dream.

To think that his older brother was put in jail

For some cannabis and then rectally nailed,

Since the government views herb as a crime,

Jailing these non-violent people with slime;

Hence they're raped for getting high

Even though it would make George Washington cry—

Our country's father was encompassed by hemp,

Sowing the seed but to crime not tempted;

However, to the anal drugs are taboo,

Like licking a cow's junk to make it moo,

Making these folk hate America's truth,

Which was a nation founded on freedom and couth,

Giving the citizens a right to amuse

And allow their minds mental breakthroughs,

For prohibition wends a wave

That makes Americans again like many a slave;

Hence, some position themselves in cultural sleaze

Because it's the place where liberty does breathe,

But to tax drugs and thieve away money from Mr. Dealer

Makes our country more sublime and clearer—

Feeling euphoria should not be illegal,

For does not sex and hamburgers release the same evil

That is being high and floating above

Like Noah's release of the platinum dove?

And while Noah was told by God to be sober,

King David for wine and herb did motor;

Also, his son Solomon does say

Give them intoxication to uplift their way;

Moreover, like Sam Adams did Jesus brew liquor,

Probably a chardonnay type unearthly elixir,

But of course John the Baptist was never skunked or made loopy;

At the same time, neither was Snoopy.

Prohibition makes fools rich during wartime,

Murdering and imprisoning the sometimes sublime—

Carl Sagan smoked weed to math and linguistics create,

But we'd be criminals to follow at his rate,

And what of the Prozac family and its stealth psychotropic smile

That makes men zombies and less creatively agile;

Thus we must give freedom a chance,

Remembering that Doc Holliday did not with morphine dance

Though it was available to his sharp mind,

He preferred the jubilation of whiskey designed

With more kick and could make a college girl pass out,

But if she burned a blunt there would be no doubt

That some frat boys wouldn't rape her smile,

But the booze did knock her out for a while.

Also, there's Lincoln with his big ass hat,

Being honest as a saint as a matter of fact,

Yet he shot down prohibition as evil indeed,

Saying that it stole from liberty's meed.

Truth be told our country is not free,

For there are people like Sean Hannity

Who want to imprison young men for a high,

Sending them to jail where the get raped and cry,

But of course physicians can prescribe some stuff;

However, with the feds in their face it can be damn tough;

Hence to even get good cough medicine in your home,

You may just have to endure congestion and moan,

And because drugs are illegal too,

Underground wizards find a way to glue

Pieces of shit to form crap like crystal methane,

Which jerks wouldn't use if herb wasn't profane.

To think our forefathers wanted a country so free

And that it would be thieved away by Fascist glee;

Moreover, Jelly Roll does weep

Mercurially into pain so deep—

* * * * * *

Mr. Sean Hannity, do you agree with God on everything?

Then you are perfect;

However, if God gets in the way of freedom;

Then He is not perfect, but liberty is.

ONE:

The moon was shimmering like neon cheese,

And Mahomet on a chaise lounge was enjoying the breeze,

Being an illiterate poet upon the desert floor

Until the arch-angel Gabriel opened the door

To Mahomet's mind, giving him prophetic literacy;

Plus, now did the Hebrew God he fancy;

Indeed, Muslims get the scoop from the Jews,

As well as Christians armed with the Good News,

Meaning there's a Trinity in the Holy Land,

Bragging of different theologies never bland;

However much in common does this Trinity share,

For all was architected by Adam's infusion with air

Through the nostrils until consciousness came alive,

Giving the first man a spirit to thrive

And grow, full of faith

Till Jerusalem is now haunted by many a wraith,

For Judaism, Christianity, and Islam too

Have killed each other because they foolishly argue;

Thus, what to do in the Holy Land

In order for peace to make a stand,

Lasting out of trust and hope,

May God bless us with a magnanimous Pope,

And may Caliphs be filled with the Holy Ghost,

Giving them compassion to cross the moat

And embrace a Jew for the sake of being RIGHT,

Knowing their religion is from Ishmael's might,

Which means there's more than spirituality here,

For from the seed of a Jew did Islam appear,

And Jesus did birth Christians alive

With the truth of his Jewish eyes;

Hence the Trinity was Hebrew spawned,

And "No" my brothers, this ain't no con.

TWO:

(Within the luxury of a suburban stronghold, anchored upon the American floor, sits a pre-pubescent boy dubbed Jelly Roll, him having mystical communication with the Virgin Mother, her emboldened with bright azure.)

JELLY ROLL

The first part of Mahomet's life was so calm, for he was a poet of the desert, being a handsome loafer of sorts; then SHAZAM! It's like God sends him Gabriel with words from an empyreal place.

MARY

Yes young one; however, what of the second half of his life?

JELLY ROLL

Yes I know—it's filled with gore and sex; nonetheless, King David's life had much blood and guts. Also, there was sex—lots and lots of sex. Still, look how much David loved the God of Israel. He was never tempted by the thaumaturgy of alien lands. Verily, he loved God—was a maniac when it came to loving God. Had an insane love for God that no other man could match. So, Mahomet too could still have had a life filled with sanguine sexuality and yet be a man of God.

MARY

We all must get beyond our sins and gel into a family, for we are all children of God.

JELLY ROLL

What you say is axiomatic. There must be peace in the Middle East.

Palestinian and Jew must share a dream instead of insults and rock throwing.

MARY

And does the young one have an idea?

JELLY ROLL

Indeed an idea I do have.

MARY

Please don't talk like Yoda.

JELLY ROLL

Sorry, I'm a bit affected by pop-culture.

MARY

And what is the young poet's armistice for peace in the Middle East? Give

ode young bard . . .

JELLY ROLL

Brilliance billows beyond boldly,

Meaning a Space Program will be holy,

Under the wings of the United States

Must every nation put its fates;

Moreover, Palestinian and Jew side by side

Within the confines of spacecraft will they reside,

Playing the part of pioneers with other lands

So that humanity will discover a majestic plan,

Uniting with each other for the purpose of exploration;

Also, this science can save every nation,

For just as Reagan wanted weapons in space

So must we with mercury race

Just in case there's aliens more advanced than us

That may have salacious plans to cuss

Our way of life,

Giving us great strife;

Hence, aircraft carriers above the Earth,

With engines blazing and torpedoes of girth,

Pointed away from mankind's face,

And towards the countenance of an alien race

Full of nefarious and wicked desire

To conquer our planet with lasers and fire—

So just as Reagan thought of such a plan,

It must come true for the future of man;

Plus, with Palestinian and Jew holding hands

In the confines of a fuselage exploring foreign lands

Would be the seed of peace;

Thus, to outer space we must police,

Having a global Federation of science and power,

Working for the sake of humanity's flower

Blossoming bright by way of evolution

As we with the Multiverse would have infusion,

Developing light speed travel

And wormhole shortcuts that would unravel

The mystery of interstellar adventure,

For man desires rapture

From gravity and all the rest,

Meaning in the celestial ocean should we make many a nest,

And if the Palestinians continue to kill;

Then, revoke their privilege to project and thrill

Themselves into the great beyond,

Which all of humanity is very fond,

For man is a creature of evolution,

Needing to transcend corporeal pollution;

Therefore, to unite in space must the world do

Or never will there be a mesh between Palestinian and Jew;

Plus, think of India and Pakistan—

This idea would also save their area of land,

And humanity would grow closer to the power of angelity,

Making things less deadly

For all of us souls on Earth

From which place we do gather mirth,

Loving the green pastures and ocean blue,

Never wanting our species to be through—

Axed to the grave by an advanced civilization;

Therefore, we must invoke the power of every nation,

Constructing a Space Program from unearthly steel,

Which to every leader does have appeal,

For all the flags would be on every warship,

Displaying Earth's power to be totally hip

And outshine an adversary so advanced,

Truly, this could be our last chance—

And again I say, the world would have peace,

For the heavens is where every man does desire to reach,

And if countries continue to invade;

Then, kick them out of the Federation made

By minds altruistic and deep,

Having the cognizance to never sleep

On such concepts so damn grand;

Indeed Virgin Mother, Jelly Roll is taking a stand

To better the world in which we live,

For neighbors should not attack but be passive,

Playing the part of knowing the truth,

And a Space Program has got the best couth,

So get the marines off the ground

And launch them like angels beyond the mound

Of desert Earth bathed in blood,

To the heavens before a flood

Of invaders arrive with oversized brains,

Morphing humanity into cripples with canes,

And even if aliens don't exist

We shouldn't be fighting our fellow man with a hardened fist,

But beyond the great blue yonder should we fly,

Giving us the best corporeal high.

THREE:

Jelly Roll was lonely, for the Virgin Mother had sliced back into the trans-corporeal world. Then Jelly thought S.C.U.B.A.—Self-Contained Underwater Breathing Apparatus. So what about S.C.U.M.A.?—Self-Contained Unearthly Morphing Apparatus? Just as after Christ was resurrected and passed through doors as if not there, so had Mary displayed control over her trans-corporeal self, fading away back into an aethereal plane. Hence, could humanity not design a suit that would allow us to be like angels? Truly, angelity might be 25,000 years more advanced than humanity. Thus, how to combat such a high level of intelligence? We need a Space Program. We need to design superior weapons and shielding devices. Too, science and religion must unite, burying their differences from the past. Verily, the aliens are the angels. Genesis Chapter Six speaks of iniquitous angels falling to Earth and breeding with women. Also, Ezekiel Chapter One clearly describes a saucer-shaped craft that had engines glowing with propulsive power before landing near the river Chebar; next, a door opens and supernatural creatures descend, giving the prophet the Word of God. Shit, why is all this happening? Why don't people connect the dots? How we were born?—Intelligent design most likely. And virgin birth is even possible with the technology of modern man; for instance, a hypodermic needle containing seed could easily be injected through a hymen and spawn a human life. Sincerely, the science of today could impregnate a virgin girl, so of course a God armed with advanced technology could do the same—it's all real, but humanity lives in the clouds, thinking God lives there too, having a big beard and causing precipitation and thunder to sound when he rolls bowling balls down the heavenly alleyway. Plus, we folk are infatuated with pop-culture—Paris Hilton is more important than peace in the Middle East. Shit, have you seen that girl's ass; indeed it's supersymmetry, trumping our ideals of love for men fighting in the Holy Land, where the lonely Jews sit encompassed by a myriad of Muslim forces that despise them and the weapons America grants their democratic autonomy. Damn't, Jelly Roll was freaked. Did this:

Daymare starting as consciousness goes,

Jelly was freaked and scratched his nose;

Then he cruised through his house,

Walking so gentle as if a mouse

Until coming to inside his garage

Where the walls melted away and gave mystic mirage,

Inspiring Jelly Roll to mimic the pain

Of Christ ornamented in sanguine bloodstain;

Therefore, did the young poet place a barbell on his back,

Strutting in circles as if Christ on the track

Towards the dreaded Calvary place

Where nails would pierce and a demigod disgrace,

So did Jelly pretend with his face

That he was marching in Christ's place;

Next, when the weight became too much,

Jelly dumped his burden and desired to touch

The Ghost of God in a paradisal scene,

Knowing the truth resides in Mary's mien.

   Jelly Roll wends his way through his house and into the linoleum-floored

kitchen. There, the Virgin Mother stands, glowing in effulgent blue.

MARY

If pride was not considered rebellion against God, my Son would be proud

of you for imitating Him being loaded down with opprobrium.

JELLY ROLL

I just don't get it Mom. Why the Muslims love you more than the

Protestants—it's a conundrum.

MARY

Surely, Islam and Christianity are siblings, both being born from the concept of the Jews.

JELLY ROLL

I just wish people knew that science can prove Christ was 50% of your exact genetic material. Verily, that was your blood and tissue upon the cross as well as your Son's. And what is more painful, to be crucified, or to watch your child be crucified? Truly, you endured more than your Son.

MARY

Don't uplift me beyond the Seed of God Himself.

JELLY ROLL

Still, my statement is a maxim. Plus, how can anybody dismiss your virginity? God touched your ovaries at the tender age of fourteen, and at that point you became His, as it is when an ordinary human male impregnates his wife. How could God be intimate with you in immaculate fashion and then allow your inviolate womb to be touched by another? For after God touched you in such a private place, you were forever His, having blessed genitalia.

MARY

The world is not ready to hear such things.

JELLY ROLL

But it's true! The world needs to know that Christ is 50% a blueprint of you.

MARY

Forty days paint a beard on a pretty face.

JELLY ROLL

Exactly.

MARY

Loving me is not what I desire, but peace to my homeland. You must

instruct all that you come in contact with that whether Jew, Christian, or

Muslim, all are children of God.

JELLY ROLL

Those that are Hindu; plus, those that admire the supernatural creature called

Buddha who fell upon Siddhartha are in such a more peaceful place.

MARY

Yes, the followers of the Gita and Siddhartha's coinhabitant are prepared for

what may rain down from the heavens. They expect supernatural creatures

to one day anchor themselves upon the Earth's floor. Alas, Jews, Christians,

and Muslims battle without having an open mind concerning the plethora of

souls who inhabit the celestial ocean and beyond.

JELLY ROLL

How will I preach this new gospel?

MARY

With ode of course. Rhapsody, psalm—it's all you little one.

FOUR:

  Jelly Roll dressed himself in suburban fashion, ornamenting his body in

Garfield boxer shorts, Nike socks, khaki pants, an olive green shirt from the

Gap, and a pair of fancy shoes that had no tassels. Next, he fished a beer out

from the fridge of his parental units and chugged it, needing the liquid

courage for the sermon he was about to give, remembering King David's

words concerning intoxicating substances, like this: "Wine to make man's

heart happy, and herb for the service of man." However, Jelly also knew

that Noah was instructed to cut down on his drinking, and every damn

Christian knows how Saint Paul talks about liquor; still, the fact that King

David and his son Solomon championed wine; plus the fact that Jesus Christ

actually brewed alcohol, and maybe a nice Pinot Grigio on top of it all,

proves the point that drinking can be virtuous, for King David, Solomon, and

Jesus Christ surely outpace Noah and Saint Paul concerning almost

everything. Anyway, adorned in his preppy clothes, Jelly Roll exited his

mini-mansion and strolled out into his opulent streets that bragged of

Reaganomics, where he walked and walked, ultimately coming upon two

elderly women armed with canes. He introduced himself; then gave good

ode, like this:

Palestinian and Jew fight like shrews,

Pointing at each other as they accuse

Without remembering God's gift to man,

Which is such a noble and blessed plan—

It being that us in His image

Might quarrel as only a scrimmage,

Yet to defend our geography from fallen angels

Made hostile from not having navels

Attached to God as human flesh brags,

For in His image the Scripture nags,

Inspiring the evil angels to our planet destroy,

Hexing the Earth as if it were a toy;

However, there is decency in angelic ranks,

Such as Michael with weapons that never fire blanks,

And Gabe is good on the horn,

Blowing its sound to us people warn

That soon we will have to face a war

Brought down on our planet so the adversaries can score,

Flipping the bird to God's face,

Them pissed at Him for creating our race;

Thus, goes a battle that we must win,

Which will be better fought if we don't sin

By way of uniting our religions so alike,

Gelling together and taking a hike

Up towards the heavens with many a space marine

From every nation on Earth's planet green,

Architecting aircraft carriers and lasers galore

So that we won't become our enemies' whore,

But strong and tall on our own two feet,

Being skilled with science that's hard to beat,

For before the altruistic angels appear

The prophets from holy texts do make it clear

That the iniquitous ones will arrive here first,

Attempting to steal our human mirth;

Therefore, we must hold them off till

The beloved angels arrive with strong will,

Aiding us in the exile

Of them nasty ghouls to a shit pile,

Which is truly where Pandemonium is,

A place where losers take a piss

And don't flush their toilets cause the plumbing is gone,

Meaning evil is a collective moron.

   Jelly bowed and cruised away from the old ladies . . .

FIVE:

   Jelly Roll delved deeper into suburbia. Ascending the hills of quasi-utopia

until coming near a country club where a golf course did reside. Upon

spotting two preppie men swinging there clubs on the fareway, Jelly

approached. The men were like:

   "Can't play out here little man. This course is for golf only."

   Jelly opened his mouth and let it flow:

The Space Shuttle is a piece of junk,

Outdated and performing in a funk;

Hence, to construct a better craft

Would help humanity longer last—

And do you remember when America was great,

Animated by souls who did fixate

Upon the Spirit of 1776,

Loving freedom and wanting to give it a kiss;

However, today liberty has died,

Buried in the ground where corpses reside,

For the Democrats cringe when you mention a gun,

And the Republicans shit Twinkies when drugs are run—

Both parties afraid of the truth

That haunted this land during its time of youth,

When Washington cropped the Indian seed,

And with a firearm did the Redcoats recede;

Still, today liberty is dead,

For the politicians do freedom dread,

Constructing their best theocracy

Though God gave man free will so deadly.

And the Wild West was America's greatest time,

When cowboys packed pistols, living in their prime,

But Doc Holliday didn't morphine drink

Though it was legal to every hero and fink,

But today drugs place you in jail,

Where you'll get raped up freedom's tail

So that moralists can sleep better at night,

Crafting laws that are unjust and uptight.

To think that cannabis can get you screwed

Up the ass in prisons tabooed,

And decent cough medicine you can't get prescribed,

For the DEA haunts every physicians' might,

So goes prohibition, thieving away the truth

When America was free and founded to sooth

The souls of men trusted to be

Moral characters in a loving country—

Know that the bloody scene of our American Revolution

Is being spit upon by folks afraid of freedom's infusion;

Indeed, Paine would kick Sean Hannity in the teeth,

And Washington would his sword unsheathe

If for a second liberty was denied,

For every American should live free or die,

Knowing a gun is not an evil thing,

Yet an instrument that did help freedom bring;

Plus, no other country would our shores invade,

Aware that our citizens have bullets and switchblades,

But liberals and conservatives are both alike,

Forging our future into a theocratic turnpike

Congested by traffic just to amuse,

But liberty frowns from such abuse.

So I'm sorry for singing this song,

Yet how could our liberties be stolen and gone?

Regardless, peace is number one on my mind,

For Jew, Christian, and Palestinian are of my kind;

Indeed, humanity needs to sail

On a keel that will unveil

Peace for all mankind

So that we will find

A conception of Adam ultimately free

From the poison of that cursing tree

And evolve towards God and be so blissed—

The future of our race should not be dismissed;

Hence, hold onto to ideals so grand

As a Federation of Nations united in a space plan

To patrol the Earth and search beyond

With the grace of science as a magical wand,

Waving our souls into the galactic community

Instead of backstabbing our fellow man with mutiny;

Furthermore, God does desire the deed

Of all humanity to on manna feed;

Therefore, peace should be sought by us

Instead of with each other verbing a cuss;

Otherwise, we'll all wake up one day,

Being greeted like the American Indian with much dismay

If our planet is not secured by space marines

That have the mojo to thwart Martians wearing green jeans

Or whatever the hell lurks out there

Within the celestial, vacuous air—

And to think Jew and Muslim side by side

Would give our great God so much pride

That He animated our souls to unite under Him

Even when differences arise that make life grim;

Thus, sheathe the sword and scimitar,

Bracing for invasion from a community far

Beyond our Milky Way sweet,

For the fallen angels' technology may wish us defeat,

Burning our home with fire and power,

Making mankind weep and cower

As it all seems unearthly to us;

Thus, we don't advance with a fuss;

Instead we dabble here on Earth with bullshit,

Turning a blind eye to maybe a disaster that will hit

And encompass us with technology so advanced

That our soldiers will have not a prayer or a chance,

And what a sorrowful shape would humanity be in,

Made slaves to creatures who are not our kin.

Verily, we must look outside,

Past our differences that do reside

Within our hearts because our holy books differ,

So we must transcend hate and become hipper,

Architecting weapons and vehicles in space

That will grace the souls of the human race.

SIX:

Jelly Roll's older brother was ultimately freed from jail. With a stick of dynamite and some Clint Eastwood invention—BANG!!! Put that boy on a horse and rode him to Canada where hash is not viewed as a nefarious thing; furthermore, after getting raped in jail, the dude needed some hash for his fragile psychological state, which could not be corrected by Selective Serotonin Reuptake Inhibitors; indeed, need that weed that God architected for the Earthman to use. Verily, the body has natural marijuana receptors built in to its anatomical structure—blessed be the body of man.

So, after the prison break and trails blazing to a more free country, Jelly Roll cruised back to his suburban stronghold by way of roller blades speeding him like Perseus' graced feather feet from the charity of Hermes. There, amidst what the great Ronald Reagan did for Adamkind, Jelly snatched a cigar from his father's stash and ignited the tobacco with some fire. After rolling the smoke around in his mouth, he began to imagine what could help humanity even more than he was trying, and he brainstormed how them damn vampires had been haunting human flesh since Jesus said: "The blood is the life." Thus, Jelly Roll did croon to the phantoms in his room, like this:

Vampires aren't sexy as the movies portray,

For bloodsuckers have bad teeth and are sincerely gay,

Biting the same sex on their necks,

Infecting other people with a slobbering hex;

Plus, not just holy water or a crucifix,

But a .44 Magnum or a Texas toothpick

Can put a vampire in the grave

Where they'll suffer as a demon's slave—

And what's the deal with romanticizing not seeing the Sun?

For to vacation at the beach is tons of fun,

Getting a tan and scoping a hot babe,

Yet summertime is about more than just getting laid,

For while having a relationship with the opposite sex

Is sometimes scary and intensely complex—

It's what makes the world go round,

Loving somebody whose ego is on the ground,

But college girls love vampires and fun,

Giving up their chastity to any erogenous Johnson,

When instead they should be searching for a mate,

A partner in life with whom they can pulsate,

And vampires are not loyal to just one spouse,

Wanting to sex the world and every cathouse,

For it's their thirst that drives them to be such damn slime,

Meaning they're unable to control the crime

Of killing and sexing people like beasts,

Indulging themselves in these corporeal feasts,

Yet the holy man like a Levite Priest

Can carry the Ark and never be deceased,

Having a ghost that will into eternity swim

Until the physical resurrection again uplifts him,

Forging a soul both body and ghost

That with God does gel and have the most

Of a life adorned with things divine,

Drinking true blood with Jesus and some expensive wine,

Knowing the Charismatics are mystics sublime,

Full of the Holy Ghost but never grime,

Holding up snakes as Jesus said they'd do,

But I dare your preacher to perform such a breakthrough;

Indeed, in miracles we must trust,

Never to failure should we adjust,

So when at night a vampire comes at you,

A mercurial finger to the eye will his hunger subdue;

Next, shove it further and scrape his brain,

Killing that sucker like to the Green Knight did Gawain,

For humanity must heroes be,

Morphing ourselves better and free,

Never having fear that shuts us down,

Which paints our face like a tear on a clown;

Moreover, it's true that evil does reside

Within this world in mankind's hide;

Hence, for God and the saints in empyrean

Must we evolve with a new wineskin,

Making movies where a human is sexier than a vampire,

Having a spirit of toughness, armed with eyes of fire,

For even though the angels are more advanced,

We are the image of God and truly romanced

By the supreme source in this Multiverse,

Which makes our enemies desire our halos to have a curse;

Thus, be strong and to God do pray,

Evolving forever towards heaven's way.

* *

Jelly Roll woke from a poet's nap, rising out of bed and greeted by the darkness. It was night, and he peeked out his bedroom window, scoping the big neon glitter above, which shimmered proudly, and the moon was a big piece of effulgent cheese. Curious as to where his parental units were, Jelly skulked through his house until coming to their door, which from behind he could hear the synergy of Mom and Dad snoring lightly. Satisfied that all was well within his portion of suburban sprawl, Kid Roll strolled downstairs and entered his kitchen, igniting an overhead light and taking a caffeine-powered drink from the fridge. He popped the puppy open, and with an eager mouth ingested the fuel—yummy. Then, the pre-pubescent rhymester went out into the night, sitting on his front porch, inhaling the majesty of all that was holy; furthermore, he sang:

The Genetic Revolution is on the rise,

When humanity will eternity surmise;

Indeed, man will craft a way

To live forever in the day;

Moreover, I ode to Kerouac during this night,

For his hair was combed neat and his body just right;

Specifically, he didn't need tattoos, piercings, or long hair to be cool;

The dude was like a preppie but never a fool,

Partying more than any rock star,

Yet appearing normal and with an intellect more far;

Indeed, Kerouac never needed to dress like a clown,

And his shit was way more downtown

Than any rock band member smothered in tattoos

Or armed with jewelry and sluts who inspire the blues;

Thus, to be cool and to dress with class

Gets guys the most prime pieces of ass.

Jelly Roll was happy that Jack had lived life; specifically, it's nice to know

that you don't have to have tattoos, piercings, Goth hair, or be a profane jerk

to be a bad ass. Truly, Jack had partied harder than Morrison, ending up in

his mother's house where he drank himself to death—and he was great for

it! Didn't even need to rage into old age like Dylan Thomas; however,

Thomas was a bad ass as well. Anyway, Jelly Roll just couldn't relate to the

punks and freaks armed with Mohawks and nose rings. Why? Why not

maybe? Everybody has got their style; still, Jack had the most class.

So, as the night fell further into darkness, the stars continued to shine, and

the Milky Way was Pooh Bear. To steal from a genius is not so bad, as long

as you only do it once or maybe twice. And then, the Virgin Mother sliced into the corporeal world, morphing herself present in front of Jelly's

expecting orbs. He immediately genuflected, and she smiled a liquid paper

pair of pearls from behind her immaculate lips. These two were family, and

Jelly new all about the mansion that the Holy Family inhabited out there,

beyond the Sublime Perimeter, where angels jet to and fro. So, the

conversation began.

MARY

To know that you understand religion speaks of sublimity, for what

information is more important than that of God, my Husband.

JELLY ROLL

Why do fools get into black magic? It's just invoking demons and the evil

dead, but Catholicism is true white magic, for you invoke the angels and

saints of God to do your bidding. Plus, don't people understand that the

Enemy wants humanity to suffer; thus, why go there? Why respect a force

that wishes to destroy humanity?

MARY

People always invoke me, pondering why there is suffering in the world. Of

course they should know—just as there is God, so is there an iniquitous

adversary against the cause of paradise.

JELLY ROLL

Does your Son have your nose?

MARY

Of course—I'm His Mom. So, stay sharp little man, knowing that all your words are published in heaven.

And the Virgin Mother faded back into the trans-corporeal world, leaving a ghost of azure haze that shimmered up to Jelly and kissed his cheek. Jelly blushed and again began his banter, wanting to end the night with majestic song, like this:

When Saint Joseph married the Virgin Mary

His previous wife had died and he was hairy,

Having a beard; plus children indeed,

Blessed by God with a donkey-like steed

In order to protect the Christ

From the possibility of Herod's heist.

And Joseph's children were: Judas, Justus, James, Assia, and Lydia,

And it wouldn't even matter if the dude had Chlamydia,

For Mary's womb was touched and protected by God,

And Saint Joseph was celibate giving a nod

To his Lord in heaven beyond

Who gave him a gift but wasn't conned,

For he would be reunited with his first wife

Who was graced in the cosmos with eternal life;

Moreover, know of Mary's perpetual virginity,

Having a hymen constructed by God's boundary

Much like many a Muslim believe

To inherit virgins after life will unweave

Where in a trans-corporeal harem in space,

The hymen regenerates after every thrusting pace—

But more to heaven is there than this,

For God is not just about sexual bliss.

Understand: The physical resurrection of mankind is true,

Stealing our ghosts back to bodies as does believe a true Jew,

For Ezekiel saw the flesh back on bone

When man will be reconstructed after death's slow moan;

Hence, even today from the grave

Could we clone every corpse and save

Their life to be lived again,

So could God with His technology grin

And bring back every human life

Dead in the ground like a truck that did jackknife—

Be not afraid of death,

For God's science can give immortal breath

To every soul buried beneath,

Rising like a blade shimmering and unsheathed;

Specifically, God's got the best technology,

Having biomechanical mystery—

(Even though that didn't really rhyme,

I, Mr. Jelly am not spinning poetasterism-like slime.)

So, know that the Celestial Hierarchy

Is more than Saint Paul or did Dionysius the Pseudo-Areopagite see,

Flaming with engines and medicines divine,

Conquering all cancer and morphing it benign,

So that every man can be like Jack Kennedy,

Smoking and drinking for all eternity.

Therefore, fear not the time of your demise,

For in the future those bones will rise,

Or cloned from the grave you will be

Connected to all that you once did see—

Now we cruise back to drugs,

Giving a mentor the most of hugs,

For a mentor we need to understand

That drugs aren't evil in any land,

But if used to architect art or science

Instead of carousing like a dunce;

Then, drugs are noble for the people

If used to ascend a holy steeple—

Too, Air Force pilots use amphetamines,

So with the future must we have dreams

About our body being built with receptors

For morphine and marijuana are its connectors;

Otherwise, the drugs wouldn't make you high

But they do and you must fly

With a mathematical or musical mind

Or a linguistic equation to unearth and find,

Creating a better place with your brain—

Not getting wasted and foolishly listening to Ozzy's Crazy Train;

Indeed, like sex, drugs can be bad,

Yet to make illegal their fad

Causes a black market to rise and thrive;

Plus, there is murder of good and bad guys;

Indeed, Al Capone did kill to push booze;

Also, Eliot Ness did many a man put in a noose

Until the clear mind of Roosevelt did free—

Giving back to America more liberty!!!

And what's the scoop with Britney Spears?

The hatred of her paints my face with tears;

Moreover, most chicks are just jealous of her moves,

Them not having the tail to so many guys refuse,

So let the girl claim her fame,

For she's like Marilyn Monroe having game,

And a blonde nimbus crown does suit her best,

Trumping all the other stars and their teeth white by Crest;

Indeed, the yellow-haired Britney blows away

All contenders who wish to play,

And while this has nothing to do with my poem,

If I didn't mention Miss Spears I'd surely foam

At the mouth for her hearty thighs,

For I'm so in love with her chocolate-brown eyes.

So to Britney does Jelly Say:

Reinventing yourself is the American way—

Gatsby became what he had to be,

And Jesse Ventura a zillion careers has he;

Hence Miss Spears, write a book of poems

Or think about decorating homes—

You are more than music and sound,

So search your soul for another talent found.

   The Virgin Mother reanimated herself in front of Jelly Roll, as she usually

does. The little man smiled her way.

JELLY ROLL

Mother, what will America do with Britney?

MARY

She can do anything; she has an unearthly ghost within her machine.

JELLY ROLL

If I was President, I'd make her the United States Press Secretary. Verily,

getting the dirt from Britney would make everybody pay attention to what's

happening in Washington. Yes, Britney must be the Press Secretary!!!

MARY

And I left a Coptic ascetic starving himself in a cave for this?

JELLY ROLL

Sorry . . .

MARY

You have a heart filled with love, and I am never sorry to spend my time
with you. Even I can joke sometimes.

JELLY ROLL

Life is stranger than I ever suspected.

MARY

Be not afraid, for I will fight for my children no matter what, and truly you
are a child of my heart.

And, armed with a technology truly unearthly, Mary faded away into
where her heart did desire, and just as her Son has the Sacred Heart, it truly
was constructed by her genetics mixed with the Essence of the God of Israel.
So, Jelly Roll accepted his mysticism with casual coolness, knowing of his
fortune to have Mary as a mother and friend. Then, Jelly became merciful,
remembering Christ's words about mercy; thus, Jelly Roll did ode with
apologetic spirit, giving rhythmic psalm:

Mr. Sean Hannity, debater of the airwaves,

I know that you believe the Good God saves;

Plus, Reagan was your man,

Which means that there is majesty in your political plan;

Also, you like the guns from our western past,

Meaning you have a mind that from the holster is fast;

Still, drugs shouldn't jail a man,

Getting him raped during his time in prison's span,

But tax that shit and you got health care for every soul,

Making the sick and depraved more close to whole;

Anyway, I've sang my song for liberty earlier today,

And I hope you know that TRUE FREEDOM won't bring doomsday;

Indeed, another Tower of Babel is Socialism,

But taxes from freedom creates a noble kingdom,

And to think that prostitution can also incarcerate a man

Speaks to a country where freedom is blocked by a dam;

Otherwise, a corporeally scarred man could have a night of romance

Instead of only having copulation with his sweatpants,

Weeping to his mother that a girl will never hold him,

Making his spirit dark and dim.

Verily, give freedom a chance,

Never questioning with a second glance,

For if God gave man free will,

Who are we to thieve it away cause it may thrill?

Jelly Roll wanted everybody to like him; at the same time, he had to champion the Spirit of 1776, going boldly back to yesteryear, when our forefathers spawned liberty for all men save those in the South not wanting to be true abolitionists such as the libertarian Paine. And yes, while Jelly had been tough on Mr. Hannity, it was for his own good, for the guy's radio show oozes with music blaring the concept of freedom, but far from the total idea of freedom does the Kennedyesque talk show host promote. Still, he's friends with Ann Coulter, and Jelly would like to have her cloned and be his girlfriend, her ornamented in a blonde mane of shimmering gold; however, Jelly knew that his ideas would never be accepted, for freedom is only for the brave—those with enough courage to let man live in a land of liberty. Are you brave enough for freedom? Do you trust yourself enough to let your fellow man live his life, or do you wish to curb the enthusiasm of souls on different paths than you? Regardless, man won't be shackled by theocracies without revolt. God is great indeed; however, He desires mercy not bondage. And Jelly Roll went further into the night, remembering the wisdom of Blake: "The fox condemns the trap, not himself."

EPILOGUE:

Ronnie Raygun was powerful indeed,

Being a faithful soul to Nancy—that astrological princess he married;

Moreover, he bought more nukes and freaked the Russkies,

Proving America could trump bears, even grizzles;

However, the war on drugs was a crime,

For our country is supposed to be sublime;

Furthermore, a declaration of war upon your own people

Destroys the majesty of America's steeple;

Still, Raygun is a legend it's true,

Speaking about the aliens and what we'd do

If like precipitation ambiguous

Fell from the skies armed with cruelness;

Indeed, Raygun wanted the big guns locked and loaded in space,

Yet the younger politicians did this idea disgrace,

And here we go fighting with Arabs

When we should be architecting craft like that flown by Ezekiel's Cherubs;

Subsequently, hindsight is 20/20

And the Multiverse is filled with galaxies plenty,

Which should inspire the soul of man to again be a pioneer

And beyond the Milky Way jet and steer

Our science and religion hand in hand,

Gelling the two so that we better understand

What we are; plus, what we can do,

Evolving with greatness and blessing the Jew

Whose God is that of Christians and Muslims,

Which should unite us instead of schisms.

Verily, if united in space could humanity thrive,

Transfiguring itself before the supernatural does arrive

And morph itself corporeal before our eyes,

Terrifying us lest our technology can rule the skies,

For once something alien beaches itself on the azure noon

We must be able to with quicksilver zoom

And contain any chaos that might infect

Our ability to have freedom and with opinions project;

Specifically, if humanity does become enslaved

We'll be under the thumb of an advanced consciousness depraved,

Herding us like cattle;

Thus, to become cowboys again in the saddle

And arm ourselves with fire and might;

Then, we'll be strong and able to smite

Any civilization that may wish us despair,

Able to defend ourselves and get in their hair.

Truly, our planet is so sublime,

Forcing me to forge this rhyme—

So scrap the junk heap that is the space shuttle,

And construct genius that will aliens befuddle,

For now is the time of mankind,

Us in the image of God designed.

* * * * * *

Before I go, Bill Clinton must be heard,

For he was a leader totally disturbed;

However, he attempted Middle East peace,

But Arafat would not with the killing cease—

The legend goes that Bubba got Yasser on the horn,

Cussing him with some southern-styled scorn,

For Elvis did want the Nobel Peace Prize,

Which he believed would help America surmise

That great and noble was his time

In the White House even during mealtime

When a Big Mac might be devoured,

And a buxom intern possibly deflowered;

Nonetheless, Bill knew the folk,

And when it came to Hollywood he did stoke,

Fueling the artists with smiles and hope;

Still he failed, never Roosevelting dope;

Also, he didn't inhale,

Which is an action that can birth jail;

Thus, besides an economy booming,

Elvis did nothing but for chicks cruising,

And to think his legacy will be a stain

Gives him a perverted type of fame,

Yet against the Serbs he served us well,

And with Jesse Jackson did he help thieve three prisoners from hell;

Hence, Bill wasn't all that bad,

Being a hunk for the ladies and making conservatives mad—

So goes the weirdness of our leaders

As we watch them from our living room bleachers,

And that is all for today;

Nonetheless, Jelly Roll will till eternity stay,

Whispering things bizarre in your ear,

Crafting the art of good looking in the mirror.

- fini -

www.ingramcontent.com/pod-product-compliance
Lightning Source LLC
Chambersburg PA
CBHW021343290326
41933CB00037B/690